How To Write A Non-Fiction Kindle eBook In 7 Days -- That Actually Sells!

by Wesley Atkins

Published in United Kingdom by:

LeadsClick
26 York Street
London
W1U 6PZ

ISBN-13:9781502429858
ISBN-10:1502429853

Table of Contents

Introduction

So you've (finally) decided to take the leap of 'faith' and start writing your first Kindle eBook.

Congratulations. Seriously, congrats.

Many people never get past step 1 ... and that is to make a decision to do something, and <u>invest</u> in **you**.

I know it's not easy to strike out on your own, especially in the sometimes-murky world of cyberspace but you've done it, and now you're ready to start making some money with Kindle publishing.

Let's be completely honest here ...

Writing an eBook (for most people) is not a simple process. Often, people will spend several months planning before putting a single word on paper ... and before they know it, 6 months have passed.

To me, that's crazy.

I've written as much as 8000 words in 8 hours, and that particular project netted me around $1200 in the first 3 days.

Sitting on a project for months with nothing so show for it … will get you the same results you've always gotten. Nothing.

If you have a book in mind you'd like to get up on Kindle and start making money with, you're in good hands.

I put this book together, just for you.

In this short guide my aim is to tap into your subconscious and make you realize that it's possible to get your book up on Kindle and making money by this time next week.

As much as I wanted to call this book, "How to write a Kindle book this weekend -- that actually sells"…

(A far better hook than 7 days …)

I'm thinking that you just wouldn't believe that you could achieve that. But, I'm here to tell you that it's not only possible, but people are doing it everyday, and, in far <u>less</u> time.

Once you have your research material done and the skeleton of your book mapped out, it's just a matter of filling in the blanks by using that lump 3 feet above your ass'.

I'm not an excellent writer by any means. I also came close to failing English class, but I understand just a few important principles that allow me to make money from information products and Kindle eBooks.

The most important of which, is …

Speed of Implementation

In other words: "Getting shit done".

In most businesses, you get rewarded for speed of implementation. I get my head straight, I plan what I need to do, I lock myself away … and I get busy.

Sure, I procrastinate all the time. But, you need to learn how to switch off those "nagging" thoughts in your head, and just start making progress.

Once you start, it becomes *addictive* and it's easy to keep going.

If you've never experience the "State of Flow" when you are so engrossed in a project that you're amazed at how much you can get done in a single day when you just get your head down.

Then you're in for a treat.

My aim is to get you into that state of mind and have

a book on Kindle making money this time next week.

Sceptical?

Listen.

I've been where you are and I know it's hard to take that leap of faith and start implementing. There are so many distractions online, and so many other shiny objects that come along and grab your attention.

I get it.

I'm not making any outrageous income claims here, but I will tell you this … "Kindle publishing is a truly excellent opportunity to make a passive income online".

And those that take action **now**, will be highly rewarded in the future. It just takes dedication and a mindset of delivering value to your customers. In the early days, many Kindle publishers had the wrong approach.

Their focus was on adding hundreds (sometimes thousands) of books to the Kindle marketplace that were all just PLR, (private label rights) that were freely available online, in an attempt to make few sales from each book per month.

A strategy that saw them lose their KDP accounts in

a flash.

If you focus on delivering true value to your customers, not only will you get greater sales of your books, you'll be building an audience that likes and trusts you and will buy *every* book you put out ... and in business, that is the ultimate goal.

Trust.

Raving fans.

Repeat sales.

Want to learn more?

Let's dance.

6

Mindset & Overcoming Procrastination

Before we can dive into the process that I use to write eBooks, it's important to address something that affects all entrepreneurs in one way or another.

Procrastination.

… and a "limiting mindset".

These two things can crush your hopes and dreams (in any business) and requires a huge mental shift in order to overcome them.

I struggled for years with this … but, just a few daily

habits can shift things into your favour and it's not nearly as hard as you'd believe.

When you start running your own business, whether it's full time or part time, you have to hold yourself accountable to deadlines. Even if you have a business partner, that person should be focused on building the business, not keeping you on a deadline.

But, it can become overwhelming when you realize how many deadlines that you have which can easily lead to procrastination.

Your mindset is an important factor in building, growing and sustaining a business. If you put things off, regardless of the reason, you need to work on changing your thoughts.

What's been holding you back?

If you're reading this book then you've probably considered writing an eBook at one point, but didn't quite *get round to it*.

So let's delve into what may be holding you back from writing your first eBook. Whether you've started writing one and never finished or never actually got started, you are undoubtedly suffering from a failure to "implement".

One of the things that made me hesitate before writing my first eBook was my level of knowledge. I didn't consider myself an expert.

But, that word is relative. You don't have to have a Ph.D. in the topic to be able to write a good eBook about it.

Can you talk to your friends about your topic with relative ease?

If so, then you're qualified to write an eBook. I know it can seem intimidating when you see other authors and all of their eBooks. You may think you need to put more time in before you can start educating people.

That's not true at all.

You shouldn't discount the knowledge you have. I can almost bet that you know more about your area of expertise than most people.

Sometimes we tend to doubt what we know because it's "old hat" to us. You probably know about all of the experts in your field who've been studying it for a really long time. You may even see them doing interviews online or on television.

So what.
Those guys may be experts, but so are you. You bring a unique perspective to the information because none of those experts have your life experience.

Yes, you have a story to tell and some knowledge to impart. Don't keep your personal brilliance to yourself!

It's time to stop thinking and start doing!

Think you're suffering from writers block?

Let me tell you a little secret … writer's block is a load of <u>BS</u>!

It's just an excuse for not sitting down and taking the time to write. If you need to write something, you should just do it. If you're waiting for creative inspiration to strike, you may never actually write anything.

The thing about creativity is that it's tough to muster it up when you really need it. When creativity does strike, that's awesome but don't let it delay your business growth. The only way to get past writer's block is to write.

It doesn't matter <u>what</u> you write.

Don't even read it back and edit, just sit down and WRITE!

Just let everything out. When you eventually come back to read it, you'll be surprised at how much usable material you actually put down.

That's the power of "State of Flow" … you just need

to ignore those nagging thoughts in your head, and just **start**.

I realize that advice may seem like something that's easier said than done. So here are a few quick tips to help you actually START.

Firstly ...

Get your butt in the chair!

You're not going to get any writing done if you're moving around and taking care of everything else first. Your writing <u>must</u> be a priority.

You have to put your butt in the chair and JUST write.

Until you get in the habit of writing regularly, you will have to **act** like you're a writer. Writers spend a lot of time sitting in front of their computer actually writing, ironically.

You'll find that the more you make yourself sit down and write, the easier you'll be able to start and FINISH your eBook projects.

The next piece of advice, and one that I really struggled with in the beginning is to …

Focus on ONE thing
at a time

Now don't get me wrong … multitasking is important for any small business owner, but it can ultimately be a hindrance in some situations.

When it's time to sit down and write your eBook, it's <u>not</u> the time to check email, organize your computer folders or update your social media. You'll surely notice, that NONE of those activities are actually leading to getting your eBook finished.

You have to focus on one thing at a time. Even though you're writing about a topic that you have a lot of knowledge about, you still have to sit down and organize those thoughts while making it interesting to your audience.

It's tough to do this when you're thinking about several other things at the same time.

AVOID the distractions.

Turn off your phone.

Forget about Facebook.

Cancel lunch with your best friend.

Get shit <u>DONE</u>.

Get *absolute* clarity on what you want to achieve

In my opinion, this should be *required* teaching in schools across the world. I'm "deadly" serious.

I wasted so many years of my business life because I didn't really know what I was striving for. I just wanted to make a hands free "passive income" while I **slept** and found the perfect vehicle for that to happen.

From that day forward I learned *everything* I could about Internet Marketing … but the one thing that's NOT taught in any book or course that teaches you the "tactical" stuff … is the **strategical** stuff.

When I figured out my overall strategy, the pieces started falling together a <u>lot</u> easier. I became a lot happier too, because I could see the path I was on and knew deep down what I was striving to achieve and ultimately … I could see HOW to get there.

Once you know what you're trying to achieve, your brain has the magical prowess to start figuring out the steps required to get there.

If you don't know where THERE is, then that, in

my opinion, is why so many entrepreneurs struggle with procrastination … and then, can't move forward and get "paralysed" by all the shiny distractions online.

I figured out my strengths, I know what my perfect day needs to look like in order for me to be happy, I know the steps required to get there and also … I know that if I keep making *daily progress* towards that goal, I'll achieve my dreams.

And that, ladies and gents is …

C-L-A-R-I-T-Y.

… and it's a wonderful thing.

Find it.

Write with no distractions

Sometimes it's a lot easier said than done, I know.

But it's so important, that you need to make it a habit to write in a "distraction free" zone as often as possible.

You'd be surprised at how much more writing you will get done when you can focus in on what you're doing **without** outside distractions.

You'll also want to figure out what helps you be more productive. For me ... it's music. I like to listen to pop music (very loud) and this for some reason helps me achieve the "state of flow" required to sit down for hours on end and write.

Try it for yourself with your favourite music and see if it helps.

Also, you'll want to make a point of closing all of your web browsers and other windows on your computer so you can really focus on the task at hand.

Give yourself the "mental space" to tap into your knowledge bank and create an informative and valuable eBook. One of the main contributors to writer's block can be distractions. It's tough to focus on creating compelling content when you have distractions.

Get in the zone (*State of Flow*)

Once you've gotten clear on what you hope to accomplish, are ready to focus and have removed any distractions you should be able to work on getting in the zone. This is that sweet spot where you are very focused on what you're doing and the words you want to use are coming to you with relative <u>ease</u>.

It's a great place that every writer works to get into. But don't be discouraged if it doesn't happen right away. It takes practice to get to the place where you can get in the zone. This is why it's important that you make it a point to write as **consistently** as possible.

The more you do it … the easier you'll find it to get in the zone.

Remember, you're not writing the next great novel. You're creating a product that's designed to support and grow your business. You are taking the knowledge that you already have and putting it on (digital) paper in an organized fashion.

Don't *overthink* this.

But, it is important that you make it a priority while you're handling other aspects of your business. On top of procrastination and mindset, improving your "time management" skills is important when you want to write a Kindle book.

In fact, time management is important in life overall. Once you become a business owner … you'll become very aware of how much time you have in a day and how you're using it.

Using your time *effectively*

Everyone has the same 24 hours in the day. It's up to you to determine how you use those 24 hours. If you stop and think about it, those experts that you see all the time have the same 24 hours in the day that you do.

You, and only you, decide *HOW* to use your day.

I understand that you have a lot to do, especially when your business is fairly young but managing your time is something that must be practiced from the very beginning. If you learn how to manage your time when your business is young and your schedule is relatively light ... you will be a pro at doing it when things pick up.

I know, I know. You're probably wondering what alternate reality I live in saying your schedule is relatively light. Believe me, what you're going through now is nothing compared to what happens when you've been in business a few years and you've created a few different product lines.

Your schedule will pick up as your business grows. Look for ways to organize your time <u>sooner</u> rather than later.

Since this book is to help you write an eBook in 7

days that sells, I'm going to give you some time management strategies. I realize that time management isn't something everyone does naturally.

I know I didn't.

I had to learn the hard way. But, here's some strategies I've found that work for me.

Time management strategies that **WORK!**

These are strategies that I've put to practical use and found that they worked for me. I didn't try them all at once, though. I tried one at a time and implemented them for an extended period of time to get a good gauge of whether I could do it regularly.

My advice to you is … read through this list once. Choose the strategy that resonates with you and seems like a good fit for your lifestyle and business.

Give that one a try <u>first</u>.

If it doesn't work as well as you like, review the list *again* and pick the next one that resonates with you.

The thing about time management strategies is that there are a lot of them. Different ones work for different people for different reasons … and you really have to choose the one that you find the easiest and most effective to use.

Firstly, let's talk about managing projects in the form of to-do lists.

The best piece of advice I can give you here, is …

Forget technology, use pen and paper INSTEAD!

I've tried nearly every to do list app.

iPhone apps for managing lists.

Calendars to manage my time.

The time I've wasted on technology to manage projects and time, makes me pretty "angry" to say the least.

Forget it all. I love technology for most things … and use and recommend Evernote (www.Evernote.com) & WorkFlowy (www.WorkFlowy.com) for keeping track (and filing) of documents and organizing my thoughts, but for managing to do lists …

There's NOTHING more effective that good ol' pen and paper.

Sometimes, the action of putting pen to paper and physically making a note about something will help you remember it. While I think technology is cool and very beneficial in most cases, it doesn't help us with retaining information.

There's nothing wrong with writing important things down in a notebook, day planner or journal.

Pomodoro Technique

This is something that writers do all the time. They set a timer for a specified amount of time and make it a point to write "continuously" during that time period.

Personally, I <u>love</u> this technique.

I don't get up for breaks, I don't edit my work, I don't do anything during that time, other than put my thoughts onto paper (or on the screen).

The Pomodoro Technique refers *specifically* to working in time intervals. Any time interval is fine, you just need to find what works for you. I personally, prefer 50 minute chunks.

Once I've done 50 minutes of pure writing. I'll get up, have a stretch, have a drink, and then after 5 minutes … I'm ready for another 50 minutes of <u>focused</u> work.

The idea is to dive into your work for short bursts of time. Working in specified chunks of time can really help you stay "productive" as long as you follow the advice above and avoid all distractions.

Sometimes it can be tough to really focus in on a project or task for hours at a time, but if you choose smaller chunks, you'll discover that you get more done in 50 minutes than you actually thought.

Plus, this is a great way to practice getting "in the zone". The more timed work chunks you take, the more opportunities you give yourself to get in the zone.

Remember, practice makes perfect.

Write 2 lists

We're all familiar with the ever present "to do" list. Some people do weekly to do lists while others do daily ones. If you're anything like me, your "to do" list is probably way too long to really be effective.

There we're days that I'd sit and make a to do list just for that day and it ended up being two pages long. That's really *very* overwhelming and can make it tough to get going.

So, rather than making a supremely long to do list, one of the things that really helped me, was to write two separate lists; a "to do" list and a "must do" list.

Must Do list - This list should be made the previous day, before you go to bed. These are things that **have** to happen the next day. You should incorporate the Pomodoro Technique with these tasks and give them a specified time frame. For example, "Create a table of contents for my next eBook project: 3 hours".

To Do list - This is a list of things that would be nice if you could get to them today but your world won't end if it doesn't happen. These things can easily be moved to the must do list for the next day.

Once you finish a task on either of your lists, tick it off. There's nothing more satisfying than putting a check mark next to something you needed to accomplish. I've tried to find web based programs to help with my lists and nothing beats pen and paper.

Day 1:
How to Create eBooks
That *Actually* SELL!

Once you've taken the time to get your mindset together and have found a few strategies to get past procrastination, it's time to START writing your book.

But before you start writing … it's important that you make sure there is room in the marketplace for your eBook.

Firstly … when you're creating a Kindle book, you should focus on a topic that you find interesting and have a passion for.

If you don't, you'll find yourself disenchanted with your business really quickly … and writing about something that you have no interest in, is <u>painful</u> to say the least.

Remember back to the last chapter?

Before continuing with this section, I recommend you get clear about what you want to achieve and obtain clarity on where you want to be.

Sure, there are many people making good money on Kindle writing books that are proven hot sellers in a bunch of different markets (I do too) ... and I even have a software product (www.KdSpy.com) on the market to help you find those lucrative markets, but I don't recommend writing those books yourself.

Unless you're passionate about the subject.

I see these types of books as *little* "passive income" earners for me, but they're <u>not</u> core to my business.

For books like this, I typically make use of outsourcing websites like (www.Elance.com), and I'll find experts in those subject matters.

I'll make sure they are high quality and add value to the reader, but again, they are not part of my core focus – they're just passive income earners that can grow nicely on the side of my marketing and consulting business.

There's nothing wrong if you want to go this route of creating a bunch of unrelated books for an increasing passive income, but ... you'd be wise to focus in on ONE niche area and build a business around it <u>on</u> ... and outside of, Kindle.

Regardless of which route you choose, you'll want to ensure there is, indeed, demand for your chosen topic.

Therefore … you'll need to put in some research time before you *commit* to writing, it's never a good idea to move full steam ahead on an un-researched idea … yes, doing research can be time consuming, but if you create a research process that you do with every eBook idea, you'll save yourself a lot of time and effort writing something that the market <u>doesn't</u> want.

… and there's no quicker way to lose "momentum" in your business, and become disheartened when your eBook doesn't sell.

Here is a simple research plan you can easily incorporate into your eBook writing process. It may initially seem like extra work but the more you do it, the more accustomed to it you'll become. Eventually you'll have a hard time writing an eBook without this research process.

Ensure there's *demand* for your idea

Like I said earlier, don't try to enter markets without first verifying that people are (already) buying books already on the subject.

A great piece of advice is ... "Let others test the waters" ... you want to just <u>ride</u> the wave.

So how do you research markets to verify potential?

Here's how:

Amazon Best Sellers – Undoubtedly, the best way to research the potential demand of your Kindle eBook, is to look through the Kindle categories on Amazon itself ... and see if there are any patterns to the books in your chosen category. If you spot a handful around your topic with good SaleRank (under 30k) then you can be pretty *confident* that your idea will be a good seller.

You may also want to use KindleSpy (<u>www.KdSpy.com</u>) to automate this entire process for you and quickly find hot Kindle markets for you to enter ... and analyse the potential of your own ideas.

You can also perform a few searches on your topic on Amazon and check the SalesRanks of the books that show up. This will give you another view for the demand for your topic. If you find a number of books with good SalesRank you know that there is a demonstrated *demand* for it.

If there aren't any with low SalesRank, that doesn't mean you should scrap the idea. You just may need to shelve it for a later date.

Magazines - Are their magazines in the market that discuss the topic you wanted to cover? Find them and check them out. Nowadays, most magazines have an online edition that you can read, but if not, purchase a couple of hard copy issues.

Making an initial investment in this kind of research will be beneficial down the line. You can read the magazines to see if there's any interesting angle you may want to cover, that the magazine isn't.

You may also get some great ideas or a different perspective on an idea you already have.

Empathize with your readers *(Give em' what they want ...)*

In order to create a *hot selling* Kindle book, it's critical that you get to know your (potential) readers on a deep (emotional) level. You want to have some good insight into their needs, wants and struggles.

There's no point in spending 7 days working on an eBook that nobody wants to read ... so, here's some important tips you'll need to *consider* while you're creating your eBook:

1. Find the problem they need solving - You want to "zero in" on the main problem(s) your market wants solving and provide a practical step-by-step solution to resolving these problems for them. *More on this later.*

2. Don't make promises you can't keep - It's important that you can deliver what you promise. If your eBook promises to give a simple solution, give a *simple* solution. Be aware of the title you choose for your book. It's the promise that you make to your readers. If you don't keep that promise, your book won't be well received.

3. Cut the fluff – Today, nobody wants to read a bible on your subject. They want "the essential", "the step by step", "the checklist", "the quickstart guide", … give people what they want. Don't over explain your solution. Keep it direct. To the point. Focused.

4. Choose one solution - People want solutions to problems and they're willing to pay (handsomely) for them. But their looking for one solution they can use. A solution that <u>works</u>. Choose one problem and one solution. Don't try to cover everything you know about the topic.

Give a specific solution to a clear problem. Focused books sell better and allow you to create a series of books to cover a topic.

5. Keep it short - Don't write 200 pages about one topic. No one wants to read hundreds of thousands of words on any given topic. Like I said earlier, you're not writing the bible on a given subject. You're providing a *tangible* solution to a real problem. Provide it and move on.

6. Get to the meat - Don't beat around the bush or spend too much time explaining yourself. You want to get "right to the point" and identify the problem. If you want to tell a story, that's fine. Stories help keep the attention of your readers ... but, you have to find a way to tell the story while still presenting the problem and getting to the point.

7. Engage your audience - You have to find ways to keep your readers engaged. (Like above, stories work well) Not only do you want to provide them with valuable information, you want it to be engaging and interesting.

8. Use metaphors where possible - Write creatively where it makes the most sense. Don't be overly flowery but feel free to inject metaphors in your work where possible. This also helps to engage your audience and showcases your personality.

9. Build desire and anticipation – When done correctly, this can be *extremely* powerful. If you can refer to future chapters to build desire and anticipation, do it. This creates a connection to your content, hooking your readers to you and your book ... and they'll not be able to put it down until they find out the answers their seeking.

10. Create a killer TOC - Your table of contents or TOC is the backbone of your book. You should create it before you start writing ... but, be flexible if you need to tweak it or move things around. Your TOC is what people are likely to review before deciding to buy your book. Make it count. Make it compelling. Where possible, give your chapters and sub-chapters interesting names. You want people to be *intrigued* enough to purchase your book.

11. Address their questions – During your research (next chapter), you'll find out more about your intended audience's questions, wants, needs and desires. You could address these questions as chapters in your book … nothing wrong with that at all. Or, you could incorporate an FAQ (Frequently Asked Questions) section as one of the chapters in your book.

12. Under-promise and over-deliver – Remember back to a positive experience you had when someone went above and beyond their normal duty? … how did that make you feel?

Why not over-deliver in your Kindle book and give away additional resources, cheat sheets, checklists, software tools etc. to make your customers lives easier. Do you think this will lead to happy customers who leave positive reviews and recommend your books to their friends?

You bet.

How To *Tap Into* The Minds Of Your Prospects

We've briefly touched on how to find out what your potential customers want to know ... but, let's take it up another level and discover what your book should cover to create that next best seller.

Research the top 5 best sellers – the best selling books in your market are "best selling" for a reason. Check them out. Make a note of all their TOC's. We're not going to copy these verbatim. We're going to use them as "idea starters" and combine it with our own research to create the *perfect* outline for our book.

Read the reviews on Amazon - Look at the positive and negative reviews of these books on Amazon too ... and read a few of the most positive ones and a few of the more negative ones. It's important that you find out <u>what</u> customers *enjoy* most about those books and any *complaints* they have.

The great thing about Amazon is that you will likely find a few really "in depth" reviews on either end of the spectrum. Look at them as if they're about your book and *learn* from both.

Understand what readers like and dislike - Make sure you get what the readers liked and dislike about the different books. You want to make it a point to align the content of your book with their views. These reviews will show you where other writers may have *missed* the mark.

Speak to people in your audience to get ideas - If you're not completely sure about your topic or want more <u>insight</u>, go to the source. Ask people what they would want to know and take their suggestions under advisement.

If you can't get to those people easily, don't worry about it. This is an added layer that you should take advantage of if possible but don't let it take too much time. This is where social media comes in handy. There are a few ways you could get feedback from people using social media.

Ask your community - If you have your own Facebook profile or page, try posting the question you'd like answered to see how your friends and followers respond. You could simply ask whether they would buy an eBook on a specific topic. Then you could ask follow up questions of the people that respond.

Find a group focused on your topic - There are

groups on Facebook and other social media websites that have been created to discuss a *specific* topic. You can easily find most of the public groups by doing a search on Google and choosing one or two groups to join.

You want to keep your group participation *manageable* so joining more than a couple isn't a good idea. When you join the groups, you can't do so just to promote your business or get what you want. You have to <u>provide value</u> in the group and participate beyond just asking for what you want.

This is why joining more than one or two isn't a good idea. Choose the group that's the most active and get **involved**. Make sure you contribute some before you ask for something. That will increase your chances of getting valuable feedback.

The first couple days that you're writing your eBook should be *dedicated* to research. You have to take some **concentrated** time to really get into your audience and find out <u>who</u> they are, <u>what</u> they want and <u>why</u> they want it.

Make it a point to really absorb and synthesize the information so you can keep it in mind while you're writing.

You need to make a file that you use to store and organize the information but you don't want to have to keep referencing it while you're writing "in the zone".

In the next chapter, we'll talk about how to create the structure (TOC) of your book and make it an **easy** template you can use to just "fill in the blanks" *without* having to reference any of your research.

Let's crack on.

Day 2:
How To Organize Your
Book For *Maximum* Sales

We're moving swiftly.

Congrats for making it this far and *actually* taking action. Most people don't … and now, this is the exciting part, actually creating the skeleton for your book.

So … it's time to take that research you've already done and put it to good use.

If you're going to write this eBook quickly you need to work within a structure. You need to take your knowledge and research and put it into a framework in the form of a mindmap. This framework is what's going to allow you to create an efficient and valuable eBook your market (actually) wants to read.

… and, the beauty of this process is, you'll be able to MAINTAIN a "state of flow" when writing, as all your **talking points** will be on your mindmap – which ultimately makes it onto your Word document, BEFORE you start writing.

Anyway … let's get to it.

Keep your book focused - Your book needs to focus on ONE problem and ONE solution. Don't overwhelm your readers with a lot of information. You should identify the problem and solution before you begin writing.

Create your initial title - Come up with your initial title. This could be a working title that you change as you do more writing or it could be your final title. The main thing to realize is that you shouldn't begin writing until you have a title. This way you can keep it in mind as you write the eBook and work to make sure you fulfill the promise your title gives your reader.

When deciding on a title, you'll want to model the best sellers again, and marry this with your own research on what the market wants. More information on writing compelling titles and hooks, can be found in a great book called; Hooks for Books: (http://www.kdspy.com/hooks/)

Make it easy to follow - Lay out the information you want to present in a step-by-step format (where possible). This is the easiest way for people to consume your content and ensure that your book clearly offers a practical "easy-to-implement" solution.

Use a mindmap to stay organized – like we touched on … and this is "entirely" a personal preference of mine, which may or may not work for you. But, once I've gathered all my research, I like to put together a mindmap to organize the information. This gives me a 50,000-foot view of what my book will look like and I can quickly and easily move things around as needed.

This is the free mindmap software I use all the time and highly recommend. **FreeMind**: (http://freemind.sourceforge.net)

On the mindmap I like to create 5-8 main sections, then break these down into 3-4 sub-sections and each sub section can have a bunch of talking points.

Organize your book – Once you're happy with the framework you've created in your mindmap, it's time to add it into a Word document. **First**, you'll want to add your chapters, then the sub chapters and all the talking points under each sub-chapter that made it onto your mindmap. This, ultimately, <u>reduces</u> the need for you to reference ANY of your research material and enables you to maintain a "state of flow" when writing.

Cover design – Ok, so you have your book mapped out and you're confident you've chosen a winning headline. This is (probably) a good time to start thinking about get the book cover designed.

Don't think for a second you can save money and do this yourself, unless you're a designer – leave it to the professionals.

You shouldn't wait until the book is finished to get the cover designed. It will likely take some time to get the final image. So, start taking a look at the resources below that I recommend.

Elance: (www.Elance.com)

This is a freelance marketplace where you can post jobs and have people bid on them. Set a budget for $100 and post a request to have someone design your book cover.

Fiverr: (www.Fiverr.com)

This is a website where people can post what they'd be willing to do for $5 and you can request that they do those tasks. Graphic design work is one of the more popular services offered on Fiverr. This can be a (very) budget friendly way to get your book cover designed, and I've had some great covers from here.

99Designs (www.99Designs.com)

If you're looking for a really professional cover, this

is the place. 99 Designs works like an auction site where you post a graphic design task you need doing, and professional designers from all over the world will bid on your project. It can get expensive though, but the quality is by far the best I've seen.

Days 3-5:
First Draft

It's writing time!

You've done your research, you put it into a mindmap, and you've transferred the map into your Word document to create a powerful template that you can use to just "fill in the blanks".

Remember the points I gave you earlier and use them to start writing. You have to get your first draft <u>completely</u> written before you even consider editing it. Push through and make sure you complete the first draft in its **entirety** first, ok?

You've got 3 days.

Follow these simple steps and let's get started.

- Sit down in front of your computer and start writing, by filling in the blanks of your Word document.

- Use the Pomodoro Technique if you need to jumpstart your writing process and set it for 50-minute chunks.
- Write.
- Don't make excuses. JUST write.
- Write some more.

Yep, this is a very short chapter because I can't tell you anymore than this. Now's the time to write.

Get your butt in that chair and just get it DONE!

Day 6: Introduction & Conclusion

Once you've completed your first draft, you'll want to let it sit for a day, <u>before</u> you go back and polish it up. So, today, we're going to work on the Introduction and Conclusion to your book, first.

Some authors like to save these sections for last and write them after they've got a completed version of the body of the book. However you choose to do it is entirely up to you, but having a break from your first draft will make it easier to edit later as you'll approach it with a **fresh** perspective.

Today is an easy day.

Writing the introduction and conclusion shouldn't take you much longer than a couple hours, then you can relax for the editing (big day) tomorrow.

Introduction

Remember that your intro sets the tone for the entire eBook. If it doesn't draw the reader in right away, you could lose them forever. Make sure it's <u>compelling</u> enough to keep people reading while giving them a taste of the value that's in the eBook. Even if you've already written the intro, it's important that you make sure it covers all of these different elements.

Identify the problem - Make sure you've clearly stated the problem that you're solving.

Tell the readers how your book helps - Don't wait. Tell the readers how your book will help them right away. Lead with the value that you're providing to assure them that their purchase was worthwhile.

Tell the readers what your book covers - Make it easy. Spell it out for them. Lay out what your book will be covering in plain terms.

This intro is designed to drive home the point of your eBook and present the concept that you will be covering. You could also use information from this intro for your book description. You may have to tweak it some for length but it can definitely come in handy for that.

Conclusion

This is where you punch up your conclusion and make sure the book ends in a memorable … but "valuable" way. You want your conclusion to show how the book *effectively* addresses the information that was first discussed in the introduction.

Not only are you going to wrap up the book, you're going to tell your readers *exactly* what you just told them again. It will <u>reinforce</u> the information shared throughout the book in a concise but interesting way. You want your conclusion to be memorable and leave a *lasting* impression on the reader.

Day 7:
Add the Polish

Your intro and conclusion should be properly "jazzed" up by now. You're probably tired of looking at the information in your eBook, but today, we get it completed.

Hopefully, you stepped away from your draft yesterday and just focused on the introduction and conclusion to your book. Just make sure you don't let too much time lapse between your break and you finalizing the eBook. The goal is to still finish it in 7 days.

After your short break, now it's time for you to put the final polish on your eBook. Make sure you've touched on everything you wanted to discuss. Fill in any blanks you find. Spice up areas you think need spicing. This is also a great time to do any spell checking or proofreading.

Proofreader - When you're polishing your book before you make it available to the public, the question comes whether you need to hire a proofreader or not. This is ultimately up to you.

Are you a natural editor?

Do you feel comfortable in your own proofing skills?

If you answer yes to these questions, then you may not need to send your book off to a proofreader. But you must answer with a confident and resounding yes. If you're hesitant and unsure in any way, hire someone.

Sure, this is an added expense but if you know that spelling and grammar aren't your strong points, the investment will be worth it in the long run. If you know someone that would be willing to do it for free and is good at it, get him or her to do it.

This works great if your mom was an English teacher in the past or if your best friend was a Journalism major in college. This, however, does not work great if this is not the case. Proofreading isn't something you can skimp on. It's not just about having a new set of eyes on the eBook.

It's about having a set of eyes trained to pick up spelling, grammar and style errors on the eBook.

If you don't have access to any grammar nerds or word enthusiasts, you should outsource to a proofreader.

This isn't required but if you don't spell and grammar check your eBook, it **will** be mentioned in reviews. You don't want to get bad reviews because of something like spelling and grammar.

The polish of your eBook is just as important as the other steps. You have to take the time to do this. You want to make sure that the product you sell is of the highest quality. By now you will definitely be tired of looking at these words and rightfully so.

But, consider how well your high quality eBook is going to sell. All of this hard work will *definitely* be worth it.

How to Get Paid Forever from ONE Book!

So you've completed your eBook. Congratulations!

One of the best pieces of advice I can give you is … create another one. Yes, I know its not fitting for this section of the book; we'll get to that. But, I wanted to make a *point* of saying that the best way to increase your income with Kindle, is to produce more "high-quality" eBooks.

You can market your book all day long, leverage Amazon and try to increase eyeballs to your book page … but, the best way to really expand your income is to create MORE books … and leverage your existing books by repurposing them into **other** digital courses to sell on the backend of your book sales.

This can only be achieved though, if you're building an email list from your book buyers. *(that's outside the scope of this book, though …)*

How to leverage Amazon KDP select free days

You should already have an account with Amazon KDP ... and every book you add should be enrolled into KDP select. This feature from Amazon allows you to leverage their platform and increase eyeballs to your book page by running free promotions.

You get a period of 90 days where you can run a maximum of 5 days of free promotions of your book during each period.

Which you will definitely want to take advantage of.

Why?

Because on the back of every (one day) promotion we do, we're going to **tactically** use this tool to get a boost in sales of our books.

Here's how that works.

Firstly, you'll want to ensure you get at least some reviews on your book before you run any kind of promotion. Then … you'll want to schedule one-day promotions only for your book, every 2-3 weeks.

Set a reminder on your phone of the day your book will be on free promotion as you'll want to cancel the promotion … yes, cancel it at 4pm EST time on the day of your free promotion.

Yes, this sounds counter-intuitive, but after testing the heck out of this strategy, this is deadly effective for increasing your SalesRank on Amazon.

The SalesRank on Amazon is what we are trying to influence here, which directly influences your ranking in each category.

The reason we cancel the promotion at 4pm EST. Is because this is the time that most people are online in the US … and switching your book from free to paid during this time always results in better sales than letting it run until 23:59pm.

Makes sense, right?

Don't worry if it doesn't. Just trust me.

Schedule ONE day promotions only, and cancel them "on the day" at 4pm EST. Then do this every 2-3 weeks and you'll have an evergreen money-maker for a long time to come.

Every time you do this, you'll have a boost in sales the next day and for a few days after … and you'll make more money over the year than if you just did an initial 5 day promotion and left the book alone.

You can even track your results with my Excel ROI tracker and test both strategies for yourself.

You can download my personal excel template here:

http://www.5minutepublishing.com/excel/

Turn your Kindle book into a physical version (… using Createspace)

Createspace is a publishing tool (www.CreateSpace.com) owned by Amazon that makes it possible for you to create a physical version of your book to sell alongside your Kindle version.

You'll have to get another cover created, but rather than finding a new person to do it, you should contact the person that designed your digital cover.

This allows you to sell the book at a higher price point and expands your value in the marketplace. There are some people who prefer a physical book to a digital one so you want to create a product for that audience.

The other great thing about a physical version is that it increases the perceived value of your Kindle book, as it's generally priced very low compared to the hard copy at $13.95 as an example. This priced next to your Kindle version at $3.99 makes it appear like a bargain, increasing sales.

Here's some considerations you'll need to think about before, though.

ISBN - If you decide to create a physical book, you'll need to get your own ISBN. An ISBN is a unique numerical code that is used to identify your book wherever it is sold. All physical books have them and you should get one for the US and the UK. This makes it possible for you to sell your books in the States and overseas.

Createspace can assign you one for free, but this comes with restrictions that you cannot sell the book yourself outside of Amazon.

If you want to market and sell the book yourself too, here are some resources to get your own ISBN:

Bowker (www.Bowker.com)
This is the agency to contact to get an ISBN for the US.

Nielsen UK (www.isbn.nielsenbook.co.uk)
This is the agency to contact to get an ISBN for the UK.

By getting your own ISBN you keep the distribution rights to your book. It also allows you to take your book beyond Amazon.

If you add these extra steps to your eBook creation process, it will set you up to create long term, recurring income from it. The great thing about these extra steps is that they can happen in addition to the other steps I discussed in chapter 3. It's great to have an added value for the products you create.

In fact, you could easily just incorporate these steps into your process for every eBook. This way you are setting yourself up for recurring income every time you write an eBook. This is invaluable for building your business. In no time you will find yourself with a library of eBooks and physical books.

How to "leverage" your existing content and create *other* books, videos and digital courses

One of the **best** pieces of advice I ever received when I started creating information products many years ago, was to always think how you can "leverage" your existing research and content to create additional income streams.

… and with Kindle eBooks, the very same thing applies.

Leverage your research – Let's say for example you've researched the heck out of your "tightly-focused" niche subject. Well, a lot of your research material you've already gathered can be used to produce another book in the same general theme, but focused on <u>another</u> problem and solution.

Repurpose your content – This is one of my favourite ways to get leverage out of one book. Being a part of the Amazon KDP select program restricts us from distributing the digital version of our book anywhere else … but, that doesn't mean you cannot *repurpose* that content into other formats.

The research is already done … so why not create other products you can sell on your website or other, in the form of …

- o Videos
- o Audios
- o eClass slides
- o Consulting / coaching material

Add to digital marketplaces – Now, if your technically challenged and you don't want to sell the above on your own website, you could let someone else do the hosting, selling and traffic acquisition for you.

Two sites that I've used to create an income from video courses, and highly recommend are:

Udemy: (www.udemy.com)
Skillshare: (www.slideshare.com)

Conclusion

There you have it.

Now you have (all) the tools and strategies you'll need to create a Kindle eBook that your market wants to read. You've discovered there is demand for your topic, you've tapped into their needs, wants and desires and created a book they *actually* want to read.

You've hopefully got it on Amazon and you're awaiting your first free promotion day to come by.

Exciting huh? ... it's not as hard as you thought, is it?

Yes, it takes work and a concentrated *effort* but once you've done it you'll have an evergreen Kindle book you can use to expand your brand and produce a nice recurring income.

Plus you'll have the knowledge and proof that you can create an information product for your business. That's very empowering and will go a long way towards inspiring you to try other new things to support your business.

Let's do a recap of what we discussed …

When you want to create an eBook to sell, it's important that you set aside the time to focus on getting it done from start to finish. Kindle books definitely provide an added value to your business and should be used to expand your brand.

Don't let procrastination stop you from writing. Make a decision that you're going to move forward with it and do it.

Just START!

Take the time to do the necessary research to make sure your eBook will sell. You're not writing this for you. You're writing it for your audience.

… an audience with needs, wants and desires. Find out what they are.

Create the structure of your book before you start writing it. I know that may be tough if you're not used to creating outlines but it's important to make this a part of the process.

Write your first draft all the way through. Don't try to edit it. Just write. Once you've written the first draft, go back and polish up your intro and conclusion. After you polish the intro and conclusion, dive into the meat of the eBook. Fill in any blanks to make it as valuable as possible.

Creating eBooks and other information products do take time but once you've created it once, you don't have to put that time in again. Now you have something you can sell or use to market your business. Collateral is very important to any small business but collateral that educates the audience is even more important.

Remember that you have knowledge and insight that can provide value to others.

Use it to build your business.

DISCLAIMER AND/OR LEGAL NOTICES: Every effort has been made to accurately represent this book and it's potential. Results vary with every individual, and your results may or may not be different from those depicted. No promises, guarantees or warranties, whether stated or implied, have been made that you will produce any specific result from the this book. Your efforts are individual and unique, and may vary from those shown. Your success depends on your efforts, background and motivation.

The material in this publication is provided for educational and informational purposes only and is not intended as medical advice. The information contained in this book should not be used to diagnose or treat any illness, metabolic disorder, disease or health problem. Always consult your physician or health care provider before beginning any nutrition or exercise program. Use of the programs, advice, and information contained in this book is at the sole choice and risk of the reader.